VIRTUES OF THE SOUL

Virtues of the Soul

Abiding in God's Presence

PETER M. KALELLIS

Paulist Press
New York / Mahwah, NJ

Cover image by tunart/istock.com
Cover design by Sharyn Banks
Book design by Lynn Else

Library of Congress Cataloging-in-Publication Data is available upon request.

ISBN 978-0-8091-5586-6 (paperback)
ISBN 978-0-8091-8988-8 (e-book)

Published by Paulist Press
997 Macarthur Boulevard
Mahwah, New Jersey 07430
www.paulistpress.com

Printed and bound in the
United States of America

To my wife, Pat,
who joyfully allows me
countless hours
of quiet time to write

Contents

Prologue

After writing and publishing *Caring for the Soul: The Journey to a Healthier and Happier Life*, I've been fascinated with the human soul, possibly bordering on an obsession. I do recall reading and hearing people talk about "soul searching" and receiving encouragement to "take care of their souls."

What is the soul? It is the spiritual part of our self that is invisible. The body, our physical self, has many needs for its survival and growth. As a result, our soul is often neglected. In the Book of Genesis, we learn how we were created. "The Lord God formed man from the dust of the ground, and breathed into his nostrils the breath of life; and the man became a living being" (Gen 2:6–7). Some translations call God's breath, "a living soul." It is from the breath of God that we get our life. The essence of his breath is our soul, with the purpose of keeping us alive and harmonizing all the functions of our physical self.

Once the parents—a man and a woman—conceive after an intimate physical encounter, God's breath gives their conception life. In essence, God assigns the soul as a representative to care for creation, another child in

God's family. As of that moment, the soul, like a caring mother, takes charge of the emotional, physical, and spiritual growth of the child. Mothering becomes a part of the soul's basic virtues.

When we respond to the presence of God and the creation of the human being, we are faced with another mystery that our mind cannot easily understand, but our soul does. If we wish to nurture our spiritual life, we need persistent and strong faith to understand and internalize any spiritual concepts.

The Bible encourages faith and provides answers: "Now faith (*pi'stis*) is the assurance of things hoped for, the conviction of things not seen" (Heb 11:1). Faith is the sureness of spiritual truth which is of God, and the existence of the spiritual world with all its properties—not unlike the way we are sure of the material world with all the things that belong to it.

This book, *Virtues of the Soul*, will help you to understand who you really are, as you understand the other people with whom you interact in your present life. Each one of the virtues we will discuss is part of God's endowment to the soul in every human being upon its conception. Real faith is a major requirement to appreciate these virtues. While they represent God's presence, they are as close to you as your own breath. Speaking to the Athenians, St. Paul said, "In him we live and move and have our being" (Acts 17:28). I love the song of praise that exclaims, "This is the air I breathe. Your holy presence living in me." We can literally breathe in and think of our soul and experience God's presence.

My intention throughout these pages is to help us all discern, from a spiritual and emotional basis, how our souls can provide strength and peace all the time. In some way, even with our agreements and disagreements, you and I are connected. The mysteries of the human soul have been observed and discussed for centuries. Let us keep this conversation going, not only for the wellbeing of our lives but for our entire world.

Finally, as you read this book, you will notice that I use the pronoun "she" for the soul in my writing, instead of "it." I take this information from what is written in the original Greek language; the soul is always referred to in the female gender.

1

Understanding the Soul

Deep inside each of us, unknown to our five senses, an unchangeable spirit animates, shapes, and forms our personality. It is ever-present in our life since we were conceived. Unlike the engine of a car, it functions without our consent and maintains action, life, harmony, and movement for the entire body. This being, known as spirit or soul, is our essential state; it is who we really are.

This most precious part of our existence separates us from other parts of creation and resides in our body. As our body needs proper maintenance, our soul also requires sensitive caring. When our soul is cared for, we will always feel befriended and sense companionship within. In our quest for happiness and peace, caring for the soul becomes imperative. When we observe how the soul manifests itself and how it operates, we discover ways to nurture it.

The Jewish tradition uses one and the same word, *nepes*, for a variety of functions that have distinct words in English, including *soul*, *throat*, and so on. The same Hebrew term is also applied to the creation of humankind (see Gen 2:7). When God created a human being from the dust of the earth, God breathed upon his creation and made it a "living being." It is the breath of God that makes the lifeless dust a "living being"—a person.

Explaining that God has concealed his essence from humanity, Saint Gregory demonstrates that it is impossible for those in the flesh to view mental objects without a mixture of the corporeal. We can speak about God positively only when we become free from the external impressions of things, when our guide—the mind—does not adhere to impure transitory images. Instead of splitting a person into two or three parts, Hebrew thought sees a unified being, but one that is profoundly complex, a psycho-spiritual-physical being.

To increase our understanding of the soul we can start by exploring three parts of the soul—the mind, the will, and the emotion.

The Mind

The mind is the first part of the soul, clearly shown by the word of God. The Book of Proverbs gives us the spiritual ground to prove that the mind is part of the soul: "For wisdom will come into your heart, and knowledge will be pleasant to your soul" (Prov 2:10; see also Prov 19:21; 24:14). Because knowledge is a matter of the mind, the mind is a part of the soul. And the Psalmist says, "My soul knows it very well" (Ps 139:14, NIV), indicating that knowledge and wisdom are related to the soul.

Since to know is a function of the mind, the mind must be part of the soul. Psalm 13:2 speaks of bearing pain in the soul. This pain must be considered by the mind: "My soul remembers them well" (Lam 3:20), indicating that the soul can remember things that occurred long ago. The mind is the organ to know and to consider, and these verses indicate that it is also part of the soul.

The Will

The second part of the soul is the will. The Book of Job says, "My soul chooses" (7:15, NKJV) and that "my soul refuses" (6:7, NKJV). To choose and to refuse are both decisions and functions of the will. These passages indicate that the will is part of the soul. First Chronicles says, "Now set your mind and heart to seek the LORD your God" (1 Chr 22:19). Just as we set our mind to think, this verse reminds us that we set our soul to seek and, of course, to decide. That the soul decides also indicates that the will is part of the soul. Finally, the Book of Numbers says, "When a man makes a vow to the LORD, or swears an oath to bind himself by a pledge" (Num 30:2). Here, the verb *to bind* literally means "to bind one's soul." To bind the soul implies that the will must be part of the soul.

The Emotion

The emotion comprises many things, including love, hatred, joy, and grief. The Hebrew Scriptures show us that to love is a function of the soul (see Song 1:7 and Ps 42:1). They also show us that hating, loathing, and contempt are also functions of the soul (see 2 Sam 5:8; Ps 107:18; Ezek 36:5). The emotions are part of the soul. Joy is a great part of the emotion and finds a home in the soul (see Isa 61:10 and Ps 86:4)

According to some translations, the words *desire* (Jer 44:14, NKJV) and *their heart's affection* (Ezek 24:25), can also be translated as *lift up the soul* (see also Deut 14:26; Jer 22:27). These verses indicate that the emotion of desire is present in our soul. Similarly, the Scriptures speak of bitterness, misery, and grief in the soul (see 1 Sam 30:6; Judg 10:16; Job 30:25). These three parts—mind, will, and emotion—comprise only a few functions of the soul.

As we explore the encompassing parts that the soul makes available to the body, we can consider the soul's following three functions:

1. the conscience,
2. the fellowship, or *koinonia*, and
3. the intuition.

The Conscience

It is easy to understand the function of the *conscience*—to know right and wrong, and to make choices in our life. When I think of the conscience, my mind instantly recalls the Greek singer Kostas Hatzis, who is regarded as the writer and composer of the song "The Conscience," where he sings of his conscience visiting him at nighttime and disturbing him before he falls asleep. He relates how his conscience—"she"—was again asking him questions that annoyed him. She laughs at him when he tries to convince her that he is a good person who doesn't bother anybody, minds his own business, and lives a simple life. His conscience comments on his affluence ranging from his elaborate lifestyle to the expensive clothes he owns. She also reminds him of the millions of starving people in the world. When he tries to deflect such responsibility to the role of governments, his conscience questions whether governments would even consider the hungry. But surely, he claims, their primary concern is defense and protection—owning the latest destructive weapons, bombs, tanks, machine guns, fighter aircraft, and so on. With a sad sigh, she asks him if this is what his civilization is all about.

Then his conscience fades out. But the man knows that she will return to raise more disturbing questions. But he concludes the song by noting that this is what happens to people who have a conscience. And no longer expecting nations to have feelings for the human condition, he prays, "May God help us."

Of course, all humans have a conscience—that inner voice that is aware of rights and wrongs and speaks to each one of us. But still, we shrug our shoulders and ignore the needs of others. Each one of us says, "Am I going to save the world?" Provided I make enough money and live a good life, I am content. Unfortunately, many of us who are complacent can hardly hear our conscience. We sleep well at night, ignoring that there are other people around.

Fellowship or Koinonia

Another function of our soul is *koinonia*, or "fellowship." This is about knowing our thoughts and feelings as we interact with one another and discover how to be in communion with God.

Intuition

Finally, *intuition* is a process that gives us the ability to know something directly, without analytic reasoning. It bridges the gap between the conscious and nonconscious parts of our mind.

2

Emotional Stability

Our soul is our best companion and trusted friend. She is ever-present and goes where we go, follows us where we walk, work, eat, sleep, love, have fun, suffer, and exult. As our best friend, our soul is actively present within us with affection, efficacy, compassion, love, concern, and tenderness.

Our human nature craves intimacy. We look for someone with whom we can share life as it unfolds daily. When we feel confused by the demands of life, we look around for some relief, a place where we can be quiet and relaxed, and where we can be refreshed and revitalized. Our hearts yearn for some new strength to continue living a more rewarding and pleasant life.

Negative or guilty feelings over small or foolish things we have done tend to cast a shadow of sadness over our life. Being misunderstood or rejected by an intimate friend or a relative can lead us to alienate that person or isolate ourselves. This is usually a sign that we need to take a deeper look into ourselves and connect with our inner self, our soul, and see what could be the matter. Well, where else could we look and find an answer to our problems? Could this be another challenge?

Instead, we raise endless questions and keep challenging ourselves:

- How can I be happy if I do not like my neighbor?
- How can I be happy when I am angry and bitter at certain people or at life?
- How can I have peace of mind if I tend to be critical and judgmental of others?
- What if I make demands on myself and others and have unrealistic expectations?
- How can I be content if I lack temperance, and complain and criticize every event in life?

As a therapist, I encountered two brothers not talking to each other for ten years over issues of injustice in their family. The older brother is very successful in real estate. Four years younger, his brother has not been able to find a decent job to support his wife and daughter. Now he is planning to divorce his wife. How is that going to make him happy? Sisters do not see or talk to each other for twenty years because of jealousy, claiming that the other sister has been mother's favorite.

Most reasons are silly and degrade the human character. It will take years of intensive psychotherapy for many of these clients to realize and accept who they are and their contribution to their thorny situation.

Jerry, a recent client in his early forties, came to my office for therapy. He was eager to start telling me the reasons that he needed help: "I have a conflict with my wife," he said, "and I'm feeling angry, disappointed, and frustrated. I do not feel safe expressing my true feelings with her. I just walk away angry and hurt, afraid of my wife's temper and how she tends to be explosive even with some 'small stuff.' I prefer to avoid telling her how I feel."

"Have you ever tried gently discussing with your wife the truth of how you feel about your life together?" I asked.

"I'm afraid if I ever discussed with her exactly how I feel, it will add to our estrangement. So, I prefer to distance myself from the situation."

"Jerry, I think that your mind and soul are in conflict; they are wrestling within you," I said firmly. "Feeling isolated and withdrawn from an honest admission of your feelings to your wife is not going to improve your relationship with her."

With a glow of sadness in his face, Jerry shook his head and said, "Doctor, I know you are right. That's why I'm here. I need help."

"We may isolate ourselves from people, but we can never hide from what seems to be the truth, which is God's gift. Accepting the truth about who you are allows you to love yourself as God loves you. Then your soul, whose purpose is to keep you alive and to harmonize the functions of your physical self, will rejoice, and its wrestling with your being will stop. You will feel better, and you will notice that your relationship with your wife has improved."

Our soul mirrors and reflects all relationships and offers guidance for a better and stronger emotional stability. If the soul is at peace, her presence is our best friend, contributing to our body for a healthier and more rewarding life. As we awake each day and live our life, we also enter a familiar path that our soul has laid down, paving the way toward our daily plans, guiding us, and protecting us. During this time, we realize how close we are to our Creator.

The soul is mindful that Christ may not directly answer the human questions about life's adversities or the meaning of suffering. But the soul knows that Christ caringly says, "Follow me! Come! Pick up your cross and follow me. Simply take part in this work of restoring and saving your own life. And once you do your part, then you can help the people around you."

Salvation for each one of us consists of inner peace and contentment. It is a state of happiness attained through Christ's sacrifice, through his cross. Gradually, each individual needs to take up his or her cross, spiritually uniting themselves to the cross of Christ. Saint Paul writes, "As many of you as were baptized into Christ have clothed yourselves with Christ" (Gal 3:27).

The disposition of the soul is to remain devoid of fear. It is a state of mindfulness that proposes harmony within each person and maintains lasting peace. The peace that the world proposes to give us is conditional and temporary. It may safeguard us materially, providing ample material goods that please our physical existence, but it doesn't satisfy our soul. The peace that our soul provides is beyond our human understanding. It is an inner satisfaction, a contentment that only the soul experiences.

However, to attain this God-given joy, you need to explore areas where you don't feel content and come to terms with aspects of life that are beyond your control. In the Hebrew Scriptures, we read that "the joy of the LORD is your strength" (Neh 8:10), and later, in the New Testament, we read, "Looking to Jesus the pioneer and perfecter of our faith, who for the sake of the joy that was set before him endured the cross, disregarding its shame, and has taken his seat at the right hand of the throne of God" (Heb 12:2).

3

The Mystery of the Soul

The soul is a mystery to many people, but to a believer, it is a spiritual reality that gives life to our existence. Something within each of us, far beyond flesh and blood, provides energy that sparks not only life but also creativity and emotions, guidance, joy, peace, and love. Developing an internal relationship with our soul can become one of life's greatest experiences.

Reading about Pentecost—the descent of the Holy Spirit upon the apostles—in the Book of Acts, I recalled Christ's promise to the disciples at the end of his mission on earth: "I will ask the Father, and he will give you another Advocate, to be with you forever. This is the Spirit of truth, whom the world cannot receive, because it neither sees him nor knows him. You know him, because he abides with you, and he will be in you" (John 14:16–17). When his promise was fulfilled, Saint Peter, having received *the Spirit of truth*, the Holy Spirit, spoke in Jerusalem and approximately "three thousand souls" were baptized at that time (see Acts 2).

Before we explore the mysteries of the human soul, let us consider the definition of *soul* from Merriam-Webster's Dictionary, which states,

> The spiritual principle embodied in human beings, all rational and spiritual beings, or the universe.

This definition may serve as a baseline for uncovering the mysteries that lie beneath our everyday life: "spiritual part," "moral and emotional desire" "the ability to feel and appreciate—perception" and, of course, what happens to the soul after we die. These are weighty topics for any human mind to comprehend.

With noble intentions many writers over the centuries have explored matters of the human soul. Personally, I'm not a preacher, and the less I preach, the more likely I am to be heard. I'm a psychotherapist, one with genuine compassion and kindness, and more a soul mentor that paves the way for healing and provides glimpses of our lifelong journey. The curing of the soul is God's prerogative. Respectfully, I must admit that I don't have all the answers. Yet I will share my understanding of the following topics:

Spirituality

Our soul considers spirituality as rooted in the basic principle of what is going on within us. However, it is better thought of as a dimension of human experience without boundaries. The soul does not equate spirituality with a religion or as a philosophical system. Rather, she considers spirituality as something free of institutional structures and hierarchies, unrelated to dogma, beliefs, attitudes, values, and practices. It's with gentleness that the soul motivates us at the deepest level, influencing how we think, feel, and behave, helping us find a true and useful place in our life, community, culture, and in the world.

Moral and Emotional Desire

The soul is aware that good and evil walk hand in hand with each other, but that evil eventually is defeated. The global COVID-19 pandemic, for example, helped many of us to see the world in a different perspective. Bishops, priests, rabbis, and ministers from different churches and temples featured services and offered messages of comfort and support toward the world's scared and most concerned populations. Several television programs, radio shows, and social media turned our attention, not to medical professionals or research scientists working diligently in their laboratories, but to God, through fervent prayer, stronger faith, and hope. After some anxiety and compulsory isolations, several comforting observations appeared on my computer screen that brought hope.

Furthermore, anger, boredom, conflicts, and depression—these negative feelings—cause problems to our human nature. It is the soul that is alert and expresses God's love and comfort as the soul represents what makes human lives active and bearable.

Perceptions

Every human being develops a gradual and different perception of life and what it is about. The soul being ever-present in our lives brings God's light upon each person so that she or he is enlightened and can follow the path that leads to the source of light that is our salvation, our Lord Jesus Christ.

Life Everlasting

It is our human desire to live forever. All of us struggle with the same desire, *longevity*, yet we want to know what happens after our earthly life comes to an end.

In the Book of Revelation, we read,

> Then I saw a new heaven and a new earth; for the first heaven and the first earth had passed away, and the sea was no more. And I saw the holy city, the new Jerusalem, coming down out of heaven from God, prepared as a bride adorned for her husband. And I heard a loud voice from the throne saying,
>
> "See, the home of God is among mortals.
> He will dwell with them;

they will be his peoples,
and God himself will be with them;
he will wipe every tear from their eyes.
Death will be no more;
mourning and crying and pain will be no more,
for the first things have passed away." (Rev 21:1–4)

Many people are familiar with the words of Jesus, "What will it profit them if they gain the whole world but forfeit their life?" (Matt 16:26; see also Mark 8:36). And the words attributed to Mahatma Gandhi, "Prayer is not asking. It is a longing of the soul."

Thomas Moore in his book, *Care of the Soul*, offers "a program for bringing soul back into life."[1] What does he mean by soul? He writes, "Soul is not a thing but a quality or dimension of experiencing life and ourselves. It has to do with depth, value, relatedness, heart and personal substance." For him, soul is the seat of the emotions and the hub of our lives. He claims that a loss of soul lies behind the restlessness, addiction, anger, insecurity, and frustration of so many contemporary men and women. With lives devoid of meaning and purpose, people yearn for something to nourish their souls. "The great malady of the twentieth century," he writes, "implicated in all of our troubles and affecting us individually and socially, is 'loss of soul.' When soul is neglected, it doesn't just go away; it appears symptomatically in obsessions, addictions, violence

1. Thomas Moore, *Care of the Soul: A Guide for Cultivating Depth and Sacredness in Everyday Life* (New York: HarperCollins, 1992), xiv.

and loss of meaning"[2]—all symptoms that send patients to therapists. He has provided a recipe for soulful living in troubled times. He helps us see that we can survive and learn from our personal troubles, tragedies, and follies. He proclaims that soul cannot be separated from body, family, work, love, or power. And by challenging us to care for our souls, Moore draws a bead on the bounties of spirituality. In the end, he calls us to our true vocation in life, which is to care for the world's soul. *Care of the Soul* is an essential primer for those who want to relate spiritually as they interact with others in their everyday life.

If the soul's capacity of keeping our physical functions in harmony is not honored, the soul will want to return to its Creator. It could be argued that no age has been exempt from the loss of soul, but this century's loss is compounded further by our ignorance of what the soul is. Because the soul has been waxed, polished, and overlaid with so many theological abstract finishes through the ages, the mind, the intellect, and the ego often resist and oppose it. Consequently, we are left with the option to concede the idea that "it is impossible to define precisely what the soul is." If we are to learn more about the soul, we must accept complexity and the darker side of our human nature. "If we want to live from our depths—soulfully—then we will have to give up all pretenses to innocence."[3] The soul reveals herself most easily in those places where we feel inferior, limited in our perceptions, and humble.

---

2. Moore, *Care of the Soul*, xi.
3. Moore, *Care of the Soul*, 136.

4

Your Relationship with Your Soul

When we ask, "What is the soul?" it is like asking questions such as, "What is God?," "What is love or justice?," "What is a spirit?," and "What is the air we breathe?" Can anyone really understand the mystery of the incarnation—how, out of infinite love, God became a human being and appeared into the world as Jesus Christ? These are abstract concepts and, while we cannot touch or see them, we feel the results or experience how they contribute to our life.

If I were to describe the soul, I would say that *it is that invisible part of us that keeps each of us alive and connected to God*. While it has to do with things eternal, it also has to do with your humanity—the quality of your life, and how you relate to yourself and to others. Everyone has a soul, whether they consider themselves religious or not. It is the most important part of the body—it keeps us alive and reasonably functional and fulfilling our purpose.

Furthermore, your relationship with your soul is more than just what makes you feel alive and healthy. It is also caring by providing physical comfort, like buying a quality bed and mattress that make your aching body feel better after a good night's sleep. This is a simple example, yet important because your investment can relieve your body from pains and aches.

It helps to be ever mindful that you are a human being with a soul in search of a longer, healthier, and more rewarding life. When you work diligently to meet your daily plans or your personal goals, your soul is content. You don't have to be religious or doing something overtly spiritual for this to happen. Your soul maintains your life whether you acknowledge its presence or not. The soul invites us to look upon our current life with the vision that is sacred, helping us to *reverence* and cherish our interaction with people in our everyday life.

When certain experiences that you are going through help you and strengthen your connection with God, you know that your soul has been an active participant. You may not be aware that this is what is happening, because your soul's presence is invisible to you. Yet, there is never a single moment that your soul is absent from your life. It is ever active within you as you take in each breath; without that breath the body dies. Just as we cannot live without oxygen, our soul is the oxygen of our life.

As two friends interact with reciprocal love and concern for each other's wellness, their love becomes stronger. Such an understanding of a relationship with our soul allows us to better approach what our spiritual life could be. This also includes our task of bringing help to our brothers or sisters in need. As our soul embraces all people with affection and care, she teaches us how to live our lives in accordance with the divine will, wishing us to have a proper relationship with Jesus Christ, our God and Savior. A strong and meaningful relationship with Jesus is what we call the experience of *salvation*. But what is salvation?

Religious people often speak of "being saved," "getting saved," "getting salvation," or "receiving their reward." What does this mean? *As Christians we want salvation.* Most of us hope that, when the time comes to leave this earthly life, we will transition to a better one.

In some cultures, salvation is no different from being saved from a burning house, an overturned car, a raging river, or some other dangerous predicament from which one cannot escape. Being saved means being *delivered* from a fate that, without intervention by another party, would result in injury or death. It means being *preserved*. Being saved, in the religious sense, however, involves deliverance, preservation, and redemption.

God's true meaning of salvation is not simply being delivered from death, but also living a life enriched with the gifts of the Holy Spirit—genuine love, lasting joy, and peace. Salvation cannot be earned—it is a gift freely given by God. There is absolutely nothing that average people or believers of the Christian faith can do to merit or earn it. My mention of the word *salvation* is not to convert anyone to my religious background, for salvation is God's gift to all humans who believe in Jesus Christ as their Savior.

I feel blessed every Sunday as I attend my local Orthodox church. After many melodious hymns that are chanted, there is one hymn that is chanted as a prelude to the Divine Liturgy:

> Today salvation has come to our world. Let us sing joyfully and praise the One who has risen from the dead. He is the giver and leader of our life. He has destroyed death by His death and has given us and those in the graves His great mercy.

Personally, this hymn helps me every morning to start and to conclude my daily prayers. Hopefully, you will also find it useful in starting your day.

5

The Conflict Within

I woke up early one morning, not able to sleep. It was not the first time that I could not sleep until at least 7:30 a.m. An inner conflict was keeping me awake.

Finally, some wisdom prevailed in my mind. I had to face reality and realized that I needed to come to terms with my life: *Peter, you think of yourself as a former priest, but in essence you are still a priest. Once you are baptized you are always baptized, so once you are ordained as a priest, you are always a priest. For more than forty-four years you have been in the practice of psychotherapy; it is about time for you to heal and restore yourself.*

It didn't take me long to realize that the conflict was between my mind and my soul. Beyond control, my mind was crazily searching to find means and ways to solve problems which could find happiness for tomorrow or in the future.

Recounting and restoring unhappy events of my past seemed futile. My soul has been a harmonizer. Her aim was to keep my mind in control and my physical self both alive and healthy. Being ever watchful is one of the soul's virtues that cannot be underestimated. We are aware of the functions of the mind—that it exists and is restless, always like a monkey jumping from one branch of a tree to another, greedy as it moves from one thought to another, never satisfied. Its nature is "not enough." When the functions of the body are occupied with the mind, the soul continues watchfully to observe what other thoughts the mind is going to focus on. It doesn't mean that we need to stop thinking, but rather that we cannot be completely preoccupied with every thought that surfaces in the mind.

The unseen part of myself, my soul, is God's (her Creator's) representative within me, protecting me from being affected by distorted thoughts and hurtful physical or emotional symptoms.

If most of us have similar inner conflicts between our souls and minds, we need to resolve them carefully to regain peace and a reasonably healthy life. Self-analysis, as suggested by many caring professionals in the healing arts, is one practical and helpful way to resolve conflicts.

Understanding yourself allows you to direct your life wisely, find peace, and develop better relationships as you interact with others. With the regular practice of self-analysis, you will experience growth, peace of mind, and a feeling of joy that you are alive. When challenges or conflicts arise, you are better equipped to resolve them and even find benefit from them. Furthermore, understanding yourself allows you to take control of your life, find peace and contentment, and develop better relationships with others.

With the regular practice of self-analysis, you will experience peace of mind and strength when challenges or more conflicts surface. As Socrates said, "An unexamined life is not worth living." As a therapist and an admirer of Socrates and his wisdom, let me note that sometimes we can create problems and obstacles when we over-examine our life. The basic idea behind self-analysis is that everything we say and do is motivated by our subconscious. In other words, your inner self guides your thoughts and behavior.

The more you understand yourself, the more you can direct your own life, find peace, and develop better relationships with others. With the regular practice of self-assessment, you will experience peace of mind so that, when challenges or conflicts arise, you will be better equipped to resolve them.

To analyze yourself, it may help to consider and understand how psychoanalysts view the mind. Consider the following five helpful points in your process of self-analysis. Keep in mind that *repression* refers to ignoring or avoiding internal conflicts, rather than immediately dealing with them, while *dispersion* refers to the process of bringing repressed ideas and conflicts to the surface to resolve them.

Honesty

This first step is probably the most difficult one. You have worked your whole life to create the person you want to be and, in the process, those thoughts and behaviors that you don't want to accept have been repressed. Honestly evaluating how you have handled past situations and relationships is the first step to finding peace and balance in your life.

Repressed, Unresolved Conflict

It is likely that various events and situations during your lifetime have created conflicts. In some instances, you probably handled the conflicts well and they were resolved productively. Other battles, however, may have been left unresolved and festering in your subconscious. For example, you may be suffering from feelings of guilt because you once accused your mother of not loving you. Your mother has now passed away, so you still feel as though you are unable to fix the problem. This is not true.

With time and effort, you can work through the situational guilt without the person present. In the example above, by spending some time meditating on the problem, you can come to realize that not only did your mother love you, but she also loved you enough to understand that one accusation did not change your relationship.

By making a list of unresolved conflicts, you can handle them individually over time and clear your subconscious. Some areas of unresolved conflicts may include:

- issues with parents, siblings, or relatives;
- relationships that have ended badly or abruptly—both friendships and romantic interests;

- work-related conflicts;
- internal battles with yourself, related to personality characteristics and/or physical attributes that you view as unattractive, such as overeating, lack of self-control, shyness, or feeling unintelligent.

Spiritual conflicts are often related to blaming the church or God for your life situations.

Negative Emotions

Are you motivated by anger, guilt, or jealousy? Do you fly into an angry rage when you don't get what you want and feel wronged? Are you constantly worrying about making someone unhappy or do you become obsessed about perceived past wrongs? Do you find relationships difficult because you can't trust others and regularly find reasons to feel jealous? If any of these emotions are motivating your actions, then they need to be dispersed.

Blame

In your self-assessment, remember that the goal is to become healthier and happier. If you look at the list of unresolved conflicts and find yourself still blaming others, you need to get over it. Blaming others for the condition of our lives does not solve problems, it only labels them.

Often, people think that if they can lay blame, it absolves them from the conflict. Ironically, you will find that no matter who is to blame, simply being part of the conflict affects you. Blame is a trap that will prevent you from healing.

Planning

Creating a specific plan will help you take control of the situation and your emotions. Repression allows the problems to grow even if you have identified them. One way that you can actively work through your inner conflicts is talking it out (with a supportive friend or relative). Before discussing the issue, let your listener know the purpose of the discussion: that you want to resolve some internal issues and ask the listener to stop you if the talk becomes a complaint session.

Many dedicated Christians still practice the sacrament of confession as a method of spiritual cleansing. Besides feeling comforted in soul at the time of confession, it also results in finding peace of mind and a more joyful heart.

6

Guidance and Wisdom

Any efforts of the soul to provide solutions in the hearts of people whose lives have been dysfunctional are rewarded. As we each become aware of our contribution in resolving our problems, we begin to experience the dawn of peace.

Guilt

Greg, a middle-aged man, suffered from thorny, unresolved guilt over a promiscuous lifestyle. Whatever indications Greg's soul offered to his heart—God's unconditional compassion, love, and forgiveness—proved insufficient.

It was then that his soul decided to seek the Lord's guidance and wisdom. The Lord Jesus, knowing how effective the soul has been in helping people, noticed her continuous struggle to relieve Greg. He spoke gently to his soul, "I have known you for a long time and I'm pleased with your contribution in keeping harmony for the functions of many humans. Be mindful of the insidious influence of guilt."

The soul, sensing God's presence in her contact with Jesus, and hearing the Lord's gentle voice, instantly experienced an inner peace and serenity and felt comforted and motivated by the Lord's words and guidance.

Jesus asked, "What kind of emotion is guilt?" Greg's soul paused, thinking for a few seconds, and said, "Guilt and shame are often confused with each other, though they're distinct emotions. Guilt expresses regret relating to a human action. People may feel guilty over things they did wrong, things they believe were their fault, or even things they did not feel responsible for."

Initially, Greg tried to cope with guilt by rationalizing his actions and telling himself that his behavior didn't really matter. "Any sin that I committed was initially sweet for me," he thought to himself. So temporarily his thoughts did help him ease any guilty feelings. Yet, because he did not address his emotions honestly, his tormenting guilt did not go away.

Hearing the Lord's compassionate words, Greg's soul felt relieved, and after encountering Jesus, she started on that day to exert her strongest efforts to instill in Greg's heart the love, forgiveness, and unconditional acceptance of our Lord and Savior Jesus Christ.

Some nights, Greg would wake up suddenly, whenever a sin of his past surfaced in his mind. Unable to fall back to sleep, strong reminders of other sins he had committed kept him awake. Being a member of his parish council, he decided to go to the sacrament of confession with Father George, an older and respected priest at the church of Saints Peter and Paul in northern New Jersey.

In repentance and tears, Greg admitted to Father George what he had thought were his most serious sins. "After a terrible divorce from my wife," he said, "I started having casual affairs with different women—I no longer remember their names—complimenting them and telling them lies and promises to justify my sinful lifestyle. Now, I think that God is punishing me for my sinful life. In the last six months I got a nasty ulcer, and my doctor has scheduled surgery in two weeks."

"God does not punish us, dear Greg. It is the bad choices that we humans make that cause us trouble," Father George said in a serious tone of voice. "Of course, part of these bad choices are the sins that we commit, and they cause us painful consequences. Our God is a God of forgiveness and love. He loves us as a father loves his children. Even if some of his children misbehave and do sinful things, God still forgives them."

Two weeks after his confession, Greg came to accept and believe that he had been accepted as one of God's sons. He stopped being critical and judgmental about himself and felt more peace. Kindness to himself and to others became part of his daily actions. His belief that now he has been accepted and is considered as one of God's sons became stronger. He felt happier and more grateful for God's blessing.

Jealousy

It is sad how jealousy, another insidious feeling like guilt, enters many families. The first child cannot tolerate the presence of another child. The firstborn child wants to have the exclusivity of parental love. As children get older and mature, we hope they will be able to share their goods. When love is shared it never dwindles; it only increases and spreads.

Now, let us consider the problem of jealousy between two young sisters engaged in a long-term battle over a diamond ring. Since the death of their mother five years ago, the elder sister refused to get together or even talk to her younger sister. The mother had promised her ring to the younger daughter, who took care of her in her later years. The younger daughter was not in a financial position to buy herself a ring. Although the elder daughter had married into wealth and had plenty of diamond jewels, she insisted that the ring belonged to her. It was an issue of jealousy that fomented hate and rage between the two sisters.

All her life the elder sister was jealous of the younger sister, who was also very talented. Eventually, the younger sister decided to give up her ring. The other sister took the ring and would not yield. With a heart harder than the diamond, she said, "As long as I live, I don't want to have any contact with you."

Jealousy can originate in childhood when another infant appears on the family horizon. This is commonly referred to as sibling rivalry. Some parents accept sibling rivalry as normal behavior, hoping that it will eventually be outgrown. Left unnoticed or ignored, jealousy becomes a fixed habit in some human minds.

As humorous as this may sound, sometimes jealousy can also exist between parents and children. Consider, for example, the aging mother who one morning looks in the mirror and sees some new wrinkles. She feels upset. But lately she notices how her daughter is blossoming, a total woman already with wishes and whims of her own, surrounded by young men who want to date her. The mother thinks to herself, "Look at me! I invested my best years in her. What have I done for myself?"

Most likely, sons can also have subtle jealousy feelings. "Dad has everything he wants in his life, including an attractive and supportive wife, my mom. What do I have? I haven't yet met anyone whom I really like."

With God's presence and guidance, our soul will continue to combat adverse forces, such as jealousy, the reptile that continues to crawl among family members who deserve, if nothing else, some peace of mind.

7

The Soul's True Purpose

The true purpose of the soul is to give life, meaning, and motion to the body so it functions effectively in doing the work that God has designed for us. The wisdom of the soul is transformational. In other words, the soul continues to harmonize and meet the needs of the different parts of the development of the human body. The wisdom of the soul is like a compass that informs correctly what each member of the body must or must not do.

For example, if we are to climb a stairway, we must start by placing one foot on the first step. Likewise, if we want to be happy, we can begin by looking at our face in the mirror each morning and then recall that image throughout the day. The true purpose of our soul is to continue revealing God's plans in our hearts and to make God's presence a reality for every human being. "Follow your heart," your soul whispers gently in your heart, reminding you of life's purpose. These are the three important words that you must hear and follow.

As we grow older and become more mature, our soul urges us gently to let go of old, worn-out beliefs that stifle our spiritual growth, to let go of the person we were yesterday, and to aspire to be the person we will be tomorrow.

Deep within may be lingering hurts and memories etched with sharp edges of pain. Our soul smiles and blesses us with joy and hopes that we can receive strength from these memories. It is with sensitivity and a slowly evolving process that our soul points our attention toward wholeness and good health.

To understand the true purpose of our soul, you might consider writing a list of the strengths, skills, and talents that bring you the most joy and fulfillment. You may have noticed that some of the strengths you have built throughout your life have helped you overcome several challenges.

When overcoming the challenges that we face, there is often a theme to these strengths and talents that is linked with our life's true purpose. These strengths and talents are the qualities that we draw upon as we become more mature. It's a wonderful relief to realize that you don't need to be anyone other than your true self.

When seeking the key to your soul's true purpose, you may appreciate the following thoughts: your existence has a reason; you have a true purpose, just like everyone else; and like everyone else, you also have everything you need to access the wisdom of your soul, enjoy your experience, and share it with other people. Appreciating such thoughts can be rewarding in your life.

If you are a mother or a father, feeling responsible for the wellness of your children, you apply your very best knowledge, talents, and strength to cultivate joy and contentment within your family. Likewise, your soul's purpose is to bring God's ever-presence in your life that you may gratefully feel alive and honor God for your abundant blessings.

Does it seem like you may never find the key to your soul's true purpose? Have you ever wondered if you have anything truly unique and special to offer? Remember that you are a creature of this world by God's design. Your parents have conceived you, but our loving God has given you life, making you a daughter or a son. Furthermore, God is constantly available to you and helps you to grow and develop.

Dare to Be Yourself

You are who you are by God's grace. While we all need to develop some survival skills and clear out some debris, we are essentially here by God's design—a hope and a plan that no one can take from us.

You are in no way limited by your heritage, the grades you received in school, your looks, your age, or any other common measurement of success and potential. Your soul is within you for a reason—the deep desire to help you realize your true purpose in life.

Greek philosophers, such as Socrates, Plato, and Aristotle, understood that the soul (*psyche*) must have a logical faculty, the exercise of which was the most divine of human actions. At his defense trial, Socrates even summarized his teaching as nothing other than an exhortation for his fellow Athenians to excel in matters of the psyche since all bodily goods are dependent on the soul's excellence.

Some people believe that the purpose of life involves completing a task, which may be something they don't enjoy. They couldn't be more wrong. Your soul's true purpose is not another form of torture. Your purpose in life is energizing and motivating. Fortunately, there's a surprisingly simple key for knowing and realizing your soul's true purpose: become mindful of the things that bring you the most joy and fulfillment; consider the unexpected gifts, the ones that evoke passion about what you are doing. With these in mind, ask yourself how you might make the world a better place.

Our soul is cared for and directed by God, not only when we are at prayer but also when we are concerned with something else. If we are caring for those in need or doing any charitable work, we should flavor our actions with the desire and the remembrance of God's presence. Through our different spices of love, we can all become a sweet and delicious dish for our Lord. If we are generous in giving time to prayer, we will experience its benefits.

Prayer is the light of the soul, giving us true knowledge of God. It is a link mediating God and humans. Through prayer, the soul is connected with God and, in a marvelous way, embraces the Lord and is embraced by the Lord. This meeting is like that of an infant crying on its mother's breast and seeking nourishment. The soul longs for its own needs and what it receives is better than anything to be seen in the world.

As the German pastor and great biblical scholar Dietrich Bonhoeffer said to his students on the eve of Hitler's election to be Germany's leader, "I know that many of you know a great many of the hard facts of life. Today you are not to be given fear of life but courage; and so today in the church we shall speak more than ever of faith and hope, the hope that we have and which no one can take from you."

In considering the soul's true purpose, you might reflect on the idea that our soul's purpose is to make us aware that God is good and holy and all powerful. He will never abandon us, and nothing in heaven or on earth can snatch us from God's hand. Let us be reassured that our soul will continue to be present till the very end of our life, no matter what the coming days bring. As the Letter to the Hebrews tells us,

> Let us also lay aside every weight and the sin that clings so closely and let us run with perseverance the race that is set before us, looking to Jesus Christ, the pioneer and perfecter of our faith, who for the sake of the joy that was set before him endured the cross, disregarding its shame, and has taken his seat at the right hand of the throne of God. (Heb 12:1–2)

You are in no way limited by your heritage, criticisms, praises, grades you received in school, looks, age, or any other common measurement of your value. Your soul is given to you for a reason, with a strong desire for you to realize your true purpose. Once you have identified your soul's true purpose, you can become the creator of the life you were born to live. This requires a shift in perspective for most people. You are here in this world for a reason. Three questions need your attention: "Who am I?" "Why am I here?" and "Where am I going?" The responses will bring you peace and lasting joy.

8

Contentment

Saint Paul said that he was content with the ups and downs that he experienced in his ministry because he believed that God was in charge: "I have learned to be content with whatever I have. I know what it is to have little, and I know what it is to have plenty" (Phil 4:11–12).

Throughout history, people seek to be content and satisfied, but when they think they have found it, the feelings are merely fleeting. Success, material wealth, and accumulation of treasures certainly provide a feeling of fulfillment and happiness, but the feeling soon evaporates. It is common, for example, to conclude that if everyone were prosperous, they would automatically be content and satisfied.

Being content is the most powerful testimony to the truth of our Christian faith, for it expresses the truth of the ever-presence of our Creator. Genuine faith, however, leads to a life of contentment in the Lord and is a witness to your children, to your family and friends, and to the community. It is possibly the strongest witness to your trust in Jesus Christ that you can give.

It is important to consider what brings contentment to our soul. Below are ten ways that you can identify genuine contentment of the soul.

1. *An inner calmness and serenity.* True contentment is expressed through an inner calmness and peace, no matter what kinds of terrible trials and sufferings may be happening in the outside world. Many people appear to be calm on the outside, but inwardly, they are frantic and emotionally unsettled.

2. *You need to feel the pain of your suffering.* To be content, you inevitably *must* feel the pain of your sufferings. Through your own pains and sorrows God guides you in finding comfort in Christ. If you ignore the pain or make light of it, you'll never learn the lesson of contentment in Christ.

3. *You feel free to express and surrender your feelings to our Lord Jesus Christ.* It's only by committing your feelings to Christ in faith and submission to his will that you'll find contentment. Finding contentment comes through communion with Christ. Often, God uses godly friends to speak the truth to you in love, to remind you of the graces of Christ, and to comfort you in his love.

4. *While medicine may alleviate your suffering or pain, it is not a path to finding contentment.* While you should certainly seek healthy means to alleviate physical pain and suffering, especially because of an injustice, you can also find some peace in knowing that Christ also suffered as a human.

5. *Contentment does not arise from complaining about life.* If you're truly content, you'll remember that God is guiding you in your life. Some people may complain that God isn't good or wise, and they claim to know better than God when it comes to living their lives. But when we grumble and complain, we fail to rest in the knowledge of God, from whom we receive our comfort and strength.

6. *Bitterness and anger at God and others is not a sign of being content.* Certainly, bitterness and anger are natural human emotions. If we feel so deeply angry when trials happen and lash out at God and others, it might be useful to recall that God is guiding us through these trials to find contentment in ways that we may not understand.

7. *Remain focused on your God-given duties.* In times of trial, it is easy to neglect our responsibilities. We may begin to neglect family, church, or our job responsibilities because our present circumstances are painful. A Christian response to suffering is to listen to God's calling and discern a disciplined way forward so that we can grow in faith and find contentment.

8. *Always seek communion with Christ.* It's possible that our fears and anxieties become so great that we neglect our vital union and communion with Jesus. However, knowledge of Christ's love and communion with him is the very foundation of contentment and the source of peace with God and joy.

9. *Avoid dark discouragements.* When we are content in the presence of God, we remember and surrender to God's power and love, knowing that God calls the sinners, heals the sick, and gives sight to the blind. God calls us

to trust that he will deliver us from our sufferings and to remain positive in our attitudes about life.

10. *Contentment comes from following the right path.* When we are struggling in our life, we may be tempted to find comfort through ways that are not of God. There is sometimes the temptation to escape or be distracted from our trials and find an easy way out. There is also the temptation to be persuaded by false doctrine that fosters false hope of temporal rescue. It is at these times that we need to be supported by Christ and discern what is true from what is false, knowing that the former leads us to that inward, quiet, gracious frame of spirit that freely submits to and delights in God's wise counsel. This is a work of the Spirit "indoors" that brings peace and endurance.

A good relationship with Jesus brings us greater fulfillment. It is a promise. It is his desire for us to be content. But how can we be content if we are not aware of our soul's desire to keep us on the right path through our conscience? How can I be happy if I do not sense inner peace?

If we are aware and believe that we need to make some important and drastic changes in our life, but make no effort, can we be content? If we are critical and judgmental and fail to recognize our own weakness, can we be content? Can we be content if we lack compassion about people who we know who are going through critical times? Fear of being misunderstood or rejected by someone close causes us to alienate or isolate ourselves. Does this mean that we cannot have an intimate relationship? Everyone needs a relationship with another person who accepts us lovingly and unconditionally. Think of how many times we simply assume that someone in a business partnership or relationship is honest and will not let us down.

Certainly, being content does not come from getting the things we desire, but rather from feeling God's presence in and accepting our yearnings. Finding contentment is, for the Christian, a grace that comes from a heart dedicated to listening to and discerning God's will in our life. As Saint Paul reminds us, a person who has a contented spirit truly can never be said to want much (see Phil 4:11). This is Saint Paul's cordial message to revive the drooping spirits of the believers in troubled times. This text encapsulates the life and soul of practical divinity.

9

The Virtue of Patience

We live in a culture accustomed to instant gratification, where patience is difficult to find. For many young children, when they want something, they want it immediately. Parents are familiar with their children's expectations. With love and understanding, most parents respond reasonably to their children.

We have become accustomed to fast food restaurants, frozen microwave dinners, and meals being delivered with a phone call—many of these have been successful in serving the needs of busy people. Impatience propels many people to eat fast and run. But run where? When upset stomachs react, the antacid tablets come in different colors and sizes to stop the discomfort.

Given this reality, the soul's concern is our physical, mental, and spiritual condition that comes from the virtue of patience. The question is, what is patience?

Patience is the capacity to accept or tolerate delay, trouble, or suffering without getting angry or upset. In other words, patience is essentially "waiting for our Creator's response to what we really wish to have in our life."

Patience is a virtue that helps us to bear our tribulations and preserve serenity amid the sufferings of life. It tempers sorrow and staves off excessive anger and complaining. Patience is the guardian of all the virtues, for there are obstacles to be encountered in any good work, and they can be overcome only by patience.

A classic example of patience is a pregnant woman. Patiently and, at times, anxiously, she awaits the birth of her child. Once she endures the labor pains and takes the infant in her arms, patiently she undertakes the caring responsibility of nurturing and providing affection for her growing child. She is the model of all other experiences of patience.

My father's hobby was planting olive trees. He pruned them, and cultivated and fertilized the soil around them, and for a long time, he kept patiently watching their growth. I remember asking him one day when these little trees were going to produce olives. With calmness, he answered, "In about eight to ten years these trees will give us tons of olives."

"And you are going to wait that long?" I asked.

His instant reply was, "We cannot force nature to meet our expectations." His words of wisdom have stayed with me.

Recently, I reexperienced my father's wisdom, when I saw Pat, my wife, trying to grow a rosebush in our garden. She faithfully devoted time to watering and protecting it from insects. As the plant grew, she became impatient, wanting to see the flowers. When the buds finally appeared, she still needed to devote time to protect them. Eventually, flowers bloomed, and at last she could enjoy their fragrance and beauty.

I have learned from my father's olive trees and my wife's rosebush the importance of patience. Patience will keep our minds free from expectations until it is time for the "flower" of peace and joy to blossom.

Part of being Christian is our faith and the ability to accept difficult circumstances gracefully while believing and hoping that we will ultimately find resolution in God. "And let endurance have its full effect, so that you may be mature and complete, lacking in nothing" (Jas 1:4).

Patience is a most important virtue in our spiritual life, and for our survival in general. Consider Saint Paul's description of the many characteristics of love. The first thing he says about love is that it is patient, and the next thing he says is that it is kind (see 1 Cor 13:4). At the end of my morning prayer I say, "Lord Jesus, please help me, give me the wisdom to be patient and kind, for I need to grow spiritually."

As we practice patience, we find ourselves closer to God, and we become better neighbors. We become more tolerant of others' faults, more forgiving, and more ready to help others by modeling a godly life. As we follow Christ's example, we draw our strength from him.

Nowhere can we find a more perfect model of patience than Christ, who, during his passion, could have appealed to his Father to send him "more than twelve legions of angels" (Matt 26:53) in his time of need, but allows himself to be roughly bound and brought before the High Priest, where false accusations are made against him. Without resistance, Jesus accepts the judgment of Pilate, who condemns him to death. He submitted silently to the terrible scourging at the pillar, and the painful humiliation of the crowning with thorns. He did not complain when the soldiers spat in his face, knelt before him in mockery and hailed him as king, and crowned his head with a reed of thorns. Without complaint Jesus accepted the cross and bore it to Calvary, where he endured several hours of the most unspeakable torture until death. He submitted to these outrages and the many painful and humiliating details and prayed, "Father, into your hands I commend my spirit" (Luke 23:46).

Patience is tested by most people through the circumstances of our day-to-day life. When we meet challenges and adversity with patience and humility, we grow spiritually and our Lord's grace within us increases. Patience is a power sustained by our soul's caring love and God's sanctifying grace.

This virtue of patience was evident in a hospital ward I visited recently. During the afternoon, a cart arrived, bringing welcome drinks of coffee, tea, or hot chocolate for the patients. The friend I was visiting had to change beds, so I was sitting quietly waiting and observing the remarkable lady with the cart. Not only did she gently ask each person what they would like, she also spent time with them, finding out how they were feeling and offering each patient words of encouragement. It was a unique ministry of humble service which clearly lifted people's spirits.

Impatience is a symptom of our fragmented culture—and we don't have to travel far to discover it. An impatient person, on the one hand, no matter how negative or violent he or she may be, often displays their weakness. The patient person, on the other hand, endures an inevitable evil to remain focused on his or her ascent toward God. The early church fathers frequently spoke of patience as one of the highest virtues—truly an indispensable virtue. Our soul helps us to combat adversity and difficult encounters, making us mindful of God's presence.

Patience is essential in our daily lives. The absence of patience causes stress and creates more problems. Consider, for example, how many times we are confronted with situations, persons, and things that displease us and make us sad or anxious each day. Patience is important because it paves the way for a healthier and more peaceful life. All virtues owe something to patience, for without it, the other virtues suffer. However, true patience is difficult to practice because of selfishness and our fear of being burdened. It is difficult to preserve peace of mind in times of sickness, misfortune, and stress. Patience and self-control are never more sorely tested than in our daily sufferings.

Our patience is constantly tested whether it is getting up in the morning and feeling tired and weak, or wishing that you didn't have to go to work, recalling an argument you had with an associate who insulted you in the presence of a friend. Regardless of the circumstance, a wise person patiently accepts reality and carries discomforts or disappointments because they are an inevitable part of life.

Patience requires endurance under difficult circumstances. When life presents obstacles, or when our expectations are not being met, we need patience to see the results. Good things can be accomplished by those who exercise patience and self-restraint. We may have to work hard, trust, and wait, but we ought not to be idle or careless while patiently waiting.

When we pray to God asking for help, our prayers may not be answered immediately. But God never forgets our requests. God's help may not remove the load from our shoulders, but God will strengthen us to carry the burden. Patience does not necessarily exclude wishing for relief from suffering, but it does exclude murmuring about it. We need to pray to exercise patience and have courage to bear it. There are times when God expects nothing of us except silence and patience.

In the Hebrew Scriptures, it states, "Whoever is slow to anger has great understanding, but one who has a hasty temper exalts folly" (Prov 14:29); and "The patient in spirit are better than the proud in spirit. Do not be quick to anger, for anger lodges in the bosom of fools" (Eccl 7:8–9). Patience strengthens the spirit, sweetens the temper, stifles anger, extinguishes envy, subdues pride, bridles the tongue, restrains the hand, and tramples upon temptations.

In the New Testament, patience is one of the most valuable virtues of life. Increasing patience is viewed as the work of the Holy Spirit in the believer who has accepted the gift of salvation offered by Jesus Christ. In his letter to the Thessalonians, Paul states that we should "be patient with all of them. See that none of you repays evil for evil, but always seek to do good to one another and to all" (1 Thess 5:14–15). James reminds us that "the farmer waits for the precious crop from the earth, being patient with it until it receives the early and the late rains" (Jas 5:7). And in Galatians, we are reminded that "the fruit of the Spirit is love, joy, peace, patience, kindness, generosity, faithfulness, gentleness, and self-control" (Gal 5:22–23).

Patience helps us to encounter frustrations, disappointments, contradictions, privations, sickness, and hardships, without losing our serenity, and without becoming irritated or despondent. It helps us not to be upset by trivial incidents, however unpleasant, in our daily lives and to maintain peace of mind.

The saints knew how to suffer with patience, for they knew that patience in tribulation is the main road to salvation. It is easy to think that our troubles are greater than those of others. Yet a walk through the nearest hospital will soon dispel that illusion. Unless we are very self-centered and spiritually blind, we will leave the hospital counting our blessings and thanking God. Indeed, none of us has a monopoly on trouble. There is plenty to go around. There always has been. Nor does the enduring of the trials of life with patience mean that we should not defend ourselves or others against some unjust action or remind another of something that is out of line. The trials of life provide opportunities for patience and self-control, where our hurt pride would otherwise cause us to respond impatiently and without charity.

Finally, there is a difference between genuine patience and sullen endurance, just as there is between a loving smile and an angry grimace. To cherish the benefits of patience, start being patient in small things. Learn to bear the everyday trials and annoyances of life quietly and calmly. Then, when unforeseen trouble or calamity comes, you will sense an inner strength to carry you through protectively.

10

The Virtue of Truth

Truth is the fundamental virtue of the soul. It represents the presence of Jesus Christ in our everyday life. When Thomas asked Jesus how we can know the way, Jesus responded, "I am the way, and the truth, and the life" (John 14:6).

And when Pilate asked Jesus, "So you are a king?"

Jesus replied, "You say that I am a king. For this I was born, and for this I came into the world, to testify to the truth. Everyone who belongs to the truth listens to my voice" (John 18:37).

"What is truth?" Pilate asked. Pilate asked this question in jest, but he did not wait to hear the answer. He turned away and went outside to the menacing crowd and the hostile authorities, including the chief priests and the Pharisees, and shouted at them, "I find no basis for an accusation against this man" (Luke 23:4). Obviously, he did not consider Jesus guilty of any crime.

When Pilate asked the question, "What is truth?," why did he not wait to hear the answer? Some time ago,

I talked with my colleague and friend Father Leo, who is no longer alive, about this encounter between Pilate and Jesus. We concluded that Pilate did not realize or could not see that the *Truth* was Jesus Christ himself—God in human form—who stood undaunted before him.

I recall a statement on this topic of truth by Walter Savage Landor that I came across many years ago when I began my theological studies and have never forgotten. He states that "truth is a point, the subtlest and finest; harder than adamant; never to be broken, worn away, or blunted. Its only bad quality is, that it is sure to hurt those who touch it; and likely to draw blood, perhaps the life blood, of those who press earnestly upon it." The one who pressed earnestly upon the concept of truth and gave us God's definition of it is Jesus Christ.

It is imperative for our soul to learn more about truth in God's eyes. It is helpful to understand that truth can be discovered through an attitude of openness. God shows us truth in various ways. You may want to consider and reflect on the following five ways that our soul can be nourished and find spiritual strength.

1. *Creation.* We can discover God and learn about truth by observing nature and God's creation. Here, science is so important, for it helps us understand God and the universe. As Saint Paul reminds us, "For what can be known about God is plain to them, because God has shown it to them" (Rom 1:19).

2. *Conscience.* This is one of those things in us that has been hardwired by God; we know that something is right or wrong, no matter what anybody else says. Our

conscience alerts us. Saint Paul writes, "These [Gentiles], though not having the law, are a law to themselves. They show that what the law requires is written on their hearts" (Rom 2:14–15). You don't have to be a Christian, Jew, Muslim, or even a spiritual person to know the right thing to do.

3. *Consideration.* Truth is knowable. You can test it; you can experiment with it; you can prove it. If I decide to go to San Francisco and follow a map that takes me there, and the next week, I follow the same map again, eventually I conclude that the map is true. For many years, I've been following the map known as the Bible. I have found it to be true. It always takes me where it says it's going to take me. I don't always like it there. But it always takes me to where it says it's going to take me.

Often people say, "Why won't God just write it in the sky?" Why would God do that? He gave you a brain. But most people never slow down long enough to consider God's path. Most people just drift through life. The Bible tells us repeatedly, "Ponder the path of your feet" (Prov 4:26, NKJV). Spend some time in consideration, in observation. Ask yourself, "Am I on a true path?"

4. *God's Commandments.* The New Testament tells us that "all scripture is inspired by God and is useful for teaching, for reproof, for correction, and for training in righteousness" (2 Tim 3:16). A question you may ask: If I discover truth from the Bible, how do I know the Bible is true? Does objective evidence show me the Bible is true? There's a world of objective evidence—external and internal—that confirms that it is true.

5. *Christ.* The Bible says that Jesus was full of grace and truth. Truth is not a principle. Truth is a person; truth is relational; truth is Jesus Christ. When Jesus said, "I am the way, and the truth, and the life. No one comes to the Father except through me" (John 14:6), he said "I." The truth is not a religion nor a ritual. Nor is it rules and regulations. This is what separates Jesus Christ from every other leader of every other faith. Other leaders have said, "I'm looking for the truth" or "I'm teaching the truth," or "I point to the truth," or "I'm a prophet of truth." Jesus comes and says, "I am the truth."

The life of Jesus—from his birth to the very end—is also a metaphor for our soul's journey. It is time to let God transform our true selves into the new life that Jesus brought to earth for us and others. In this journey you and I are not traveling alone. We have the Holy Spirit inspiring and guiding us. And you and I have the love of God the Father, and we have the companionship of Jesus Christ, our Guide and Savior.

> "*Nothing in human history is able to equal the love which Jesus inspired, the solace which He spread, the compassion which He engendered, the hope that He kindled in the breast of humanity.*"
>
> —H. G. Emelow

11

The Virtue of Love

The virtue of love is the essence of the soul and continues to strengthen and support the rest of the virtues. When asked by a Pharisee about the greatest commandment, Jesus responded, "'You shall love the Lord your God with all your heart, and with all your soul, and with all your mind.' This is the greatest and first commandment. And a second is like it: 'You shall love your neighbor as yourself'" (Matt 22:37–39).

Jesus gave priority to love over all the other Christian virtues. Every thought, response, and act of goodwill can benefit and be effective as it passes through the fine filter of love.

In the New Testament, Saint Paul offers us an unsurpassed definition of love in his first letter to the Corinthians, "Love is patient; love is kind; love is not envious or boastful or arrogant or rude. It does not insist on its own way; it is not irritable or resentful; it does not rejoice in wrongdoing, but rejoices in the truth. It bears all things, believes all things, hopes all things, endures all things" (1 Cor 13:4–7).

Since the beginning of creation, human beings, young and old, desire to be loved. We yearn to meet someone who is lovable and who can also love us. However, we are also aware that, at times, love in our present earthly life can fail us. In an imperfect world, we also interact with imperfect people, knowing that we are also imperfect. But when we seek intimacy with Jesus Christ, our Lord and Savior, then we sense an experience of perfect love that is unconditional and lasting.

We know and believe that God, who created us, came into our life as one of us, as a human being, with a message of love and forgiveness. Mindful of the sacrifice of Jesus on the cross for our salvation, our soul reassures us that God's love is always available to each of us.

Can we make love our priority? Loving people can be difficult and loving difficult people can be more challenging and sometimes not even possible. Yet the Bible reminds us, "For this is the message you have heard from the beginning, that we should love one another" (1 John 3:11).

We spend time on what we deem important. For many of us these choices are valid: time with family and friends; work; prayer; serving the poor; striving for human rights; and protesting injustice. Yet in the Gospels, Jesus reminds us of the command and how to love:

> But I say to you, Love your enemies and pray for those who persecute you, so that you may be children of your Father in heaven; for he makes

> his sun rise on the evil and on the good, and sends rain on the righteous and on the unrighteous. For if you love those who love you, what reward do you have? Do not even the tax-collectors do the same? And if you greet only your brothers and sisters, what more are you doing than others? (Matt 5:44–47)

and also in Luke:

> If you love those who love you, what credit is that to you? For even sinners love those who love them. If you do good to those who do good to you, what credit is that to you? For even sinners do the same. If you lend to those from whom you hope to receive, what credit is that to you? Even sinners lend to sinners, to receive as much again. But love your enemies, do good, and lend, expecting nothing in return. Your reward will be great, and you will be children of the Most High; for he is kind to the ungrateful and the wicked. Be merciful, just as your Father is merciful. (Luke 6:32–36)

This is a difficult and challenging command, and one that needs to strive for total and unconditional faith so that our soul can be mindful and meet this challenge. The command is more challenging when the events of the world appear dark and there is little or no relationship with our relatives or our neighbors. In such situations, we can humbly pray for them, reflecting on their needs for wellness.

It is here that our soul reminds us of this teaching of our Lord Jesus.

When Jesus Christ tells us to love our enemies, he also offers us his love and mercy for comfort and strength. Our heavenly Father is our source of love, and his supply never runs low. When you have trouble loving someone, whether friend or enemy, ask the Father for the love you need. He will surely supply it, for it is in his very essence and will. It is our challenge as Christians to rediscover the love that Christ spoke about to his people—and continues to speak to us through our soul.

If we truly believe that God loves all of us, we must recognize that he also loves our enemies. Sometimes, we try to claim God for ourselves and for our cause, but God's love is too great to be confined to any one side of a conflict or to any one religion. God does not share our hostile feelings, no matter what offense we have endured. Furthermore, our prejudices—religion, nationality, race, gender, sexual orientation, or anything else—are absolutely and utterly wrong in God's eyes.

Jesus said, "The kingdom of God is among you" (Luke 17:21). In other words, we already have a foretaste for what is to come. Through our soul's awareness of this claim, we become attentive to what is important: becoming partners with God and working for a new kind of society where people count. People you interact with begin to matter—they are God's children like you are, and more important than things or possessions. Human life should not only be respected, but positively revered.

Our partnership with God comes from the fact that God created humankind in his image and likeness (see Gen 1:26–27). His image means that God, being a Spirit, created us to be spiritual beings. Likeness means that God, as the Creator, has created humans to be creative beings. It is through the virtue of love that our soul works in building a caring society that functions with the spirit of gentleness.

12

Life Everlasting

Does anyone really know what happens to our soul after death? Theologians and prominent spiritual writers who have studied philosophy and the Scriptures hesitate to be dogmatic in responding to this question, fully aware that no human knowledge can provide an answer to the mystery of death. And yet, we are all aware that someday our physical self will cease to exist.

The thought of dying can be scary, but it is a natural part of life. "Eat, drink, and be merry, for tomorrow we die" was the claim of Greek philosophers. Many dismiss or ignore the matter until a relative or a close friend dies. Woody Allen was once attributed the saying, "I don't mind dying, but when it happens, I don't want to be there." Although humorous on the surface, on a deeper level, it may be a subtle cover for his fear of death. However, when the philosopher Socrates was sentenced to die by poison, far from fearing death, he perceived it as his "ultimate reward."

For Plato, the soul is immortal. But the question remains, "What happens to our soul, to that part of self that keeps us alive, after death?" In our attempt to make sense of the world, we cannot avoid thinking of events that lie ahead, especially that mysterious event when our human existence comes to an end. The fear of death is a debilitating reality; it disrupts the unity of soul and body and the union among beloved persons.

For the spiritual person, the belief that death is the gateway to immortality is comforting. As the butterfly frees itself from its cocoon and enjoys a colorful field, likewise the soul frees itself from the body and finds everlasting joy in the presence of the miracle of a spectacular world created by a loving God.

The Christian View of Death

Christianity decisively defines that we possess a soul that never dies. Our death is not final. Upon death, the soul remains in a preliminary state, a foretaste of the age to come, when Christ will come in glory to judge and reward the living and the dead.

Our human perception of this reality is limited, just as our perception of Christ's presence in our life is limited. Here is where faith reassures us that, at the end of our days, God will raise our bodies from the grave and reunite them with our souls.

How can this be? Our faith tells us that if God created the universe out of nothing, if God created life and made humans cocreators, would it be impossible for God to intervene in our human history and bring us to new life? If this life, in its pure form, is so beautiful, one can imagine what kind of life a loving God has prepared for us.

Personally, I do not make any claim to be an authority on what will happen after death; I can neither ignore the reality of death nor be preoccupied with it. Nevertheless, how I deal with my death is crucial to how I deal with my life. This also gives greater urgency to the issue of my soul after life.

Often, especially when I am feeling unwell, thoughts may cross my mind, "What if this is it? Oh God, please, don't let it happen yet; I need more time. I have so much unfinished business." Then my mind and heart focus on God and I realize that all the "what ifs" can only prevent me from living my present life to the fullest. One day we will die, and we will leave behind unfinished tasks, because life is always going to be unfinished. It is better to focus on God's plan for you and trust that God is the God of the living and not a God of the dead.

Like a flower, our human life withers; and like a dream, it vanishes. But when we hear the Call, we shall all rise to meet the Lord and we shall ever be in the Lord's glorious and loving presence.

After death, my soul has already returned to its Creator. I feel no sadness or pain, yet my earthly life has ended. Despite the profound grief of my family and loved ones, I envision each of them moving on with their individual lives; they have to, because they are young and full of vitality, and I am happy for them. Life is for the living, and it is my joy to envision them advancing in life, making good choices, living long, cherishing their days, and being grateful for God's blessings.

As I realize that I can no longer control the destiny of my loved ones, I let go of my images and face the real issue: "What will happen to me after death?" Clearly, our body will eventually return to its elements. But what about our spirit—our soul? Death has no power or dominion over the soul.

> *By his death and resurrection, Christ destroyed death and gave life to those in the grave.*

In the words of John Chrysostom:

> *No one need fear death; the Savior's death freed us from it...death where is your sting? Hades, where is your victory? Christ is risen and you are overthrown. Christ is risen and demons have fallen. Christ is risen and angels rejoice. Christ is risen and life rules. Christ is risen and not one dead remains in the tomb.*

This was also the conviction of those who witnessed Christ's resurrection and went out into a hostile world against all adversities to preach about it.

It is true that death will happen to all of us some day. We are born and we die. Birth and death represent the twin terminals of life. But how do we integrate the reality of death into our understanding of life? We live with the awareness that there was a beginning and an end. The best way to deal with the issue of death is to live in a fully conscious, compassionate, loving way.

Truly, the soul leaves the body, but being of spiritual essence, it returns to its Creator. The last article of the Christian Creed states: *I look for the resurrection of the dead and the life of the ages to come.* As Christians, we believe that Christ died on the cross, was buried, and came back to life, and we anticipate an age in which we will be resurrected from the dead, and there will be no more death, pain, or sorrow, but life everlasting. Will we have a body, some identity of who we are in life after death? Yes!

Having limited theological knowledge, it suffices to say that, like birth, death is another beginning of a different life. Jesus said that we will be "like angels in heaven" (Mark 12:25).

Personal Experiences

During my tenure as a priest at Saint Sophia Cathedral in Los Angeles, California, I performed hundreds of funeral services. But one experience stands out. In Pomona, more than an hour away from Los Angeles, Eudoxia, an elderly woman unknown to me, was sick. Her daughter Eleni called and requested holy communion for her mother. Upon my arrival, I asked Eudoxia if she wished to confess. She nodded, *Yes*. The daughter Eleni, who took care of her mother, left us alone. Peacefully and in perfect clarity of mind, Eudoxia confessed what she considered to be all her sins. Then she paused. *My son who lives in Greece never came to visit me…and I miss him.* This yearning left a bitter smile on her face. Reverently, she received holy communion and thanked me for the visit. *Father, if you ever see my son, please tell him that I loved him.* I nodded, saying, *I will*, and prepared to leave.

Then she began to sing with a rather weak, yet sweet voice, *He is bright like the sun, comely and beautiful*, and she pointed her finger high in the air toward the left side of her bed. Between curiosity and wonder, I asked, *Who is bright like the sun?* With a radiant glow on her face, she said, *Don't you see him? He's right here.* I turned and looked. I saw nothing, but as I departed, I heard myself whispering, *Woman, please pray for me.*

More than an hour later, still wondering what Eudoxia thought she had seen, I arrived at my office. Venita, my secretary, anxiously met me at the door and said, *The woman who you just gave communion to died. Her daughter expects a call from you.*

Eudoxia's days ended with a simple funeral service; her daughter and a few attendants came to pay their respects. Did her story really end?

A year later, I was vacationing in Athens, Greece. One sunny day, I took a long stroll in a busy section, known as Omonia Square, which was swarming with thousands of people and heavy traffic. Casually, I stopped a young man and asked for directions. I wanted to buy recent records of Greek instrumental music.

"Sir, do you see that big building on the next block, Lambropoulos Brothers—on the third floor you'll find a great collection of the latest records." Hurriedly he moved on his way. As I walked in the direction he pointed, I heard his voice again, "Mister, mister!" He approached me as he called. "I know a better place with better prices and good service. Look over there." He pointed. "Before you get to that fountain, turn to your left, walk one more block and you'll see a very narrow alley—very busy. The third store on the right is the place. You can't miss the green sign: Records."

I found the store. It was small and could hardly accommodate five customers. A middle-aged man wearing a black arm band, a sign of mourning, stood behind a small counter and politely took care of orders. I was last in line. I asked him to help me choose a few pieces of good music. He took a profound look at me and said, "I can tell from the way you speak. You are either from Australia or America."

"I'm from America," I said.

His face instantly changed color as he said, "I wanted to come to America and visit my mother. She lived there for the past ten years. Unfortunately, she died almost a year ago." He took a deep breath. "I could not even go to the funeral—too far."

"I'm sorry to hear it," I said. "Where in America did your mother live."

"In California, but I don't know the name of the town." He hesitated and then pulled an envelope from his register and pronounced slowly. "Pomona."

"Pomona?" I asked with rising curiosity. "What was your mother's name?"

"Eudoxia, and my sister Eleni still lives there." He went on to show me a picture of his mother and sister, taken a few years before. I did recognize the two women immediately, but I was not exactly sure how to respond, until I saw the return address on the envelope.

"I know the town and have been there. I knew your mother," I said.

He pulled back and looked at me dumbfounded.

"I am the priest who performed your mother's funeral."

"You are a priest?" Now his shock was compounded not by what I told him about his mother but also by my appearance. In Greece, a priest would be bearded and dressed in a long black cassock and tall hat. I was an American priest in civilian clothes. When he heard the rest of the story, how I was called to minister to his mother and what she had said about him, he put his arms around me and cried, "My mother must have sent you here to tell me about her last days."

For a long time, I pondered this amazing encounter. Amid a crowded Athenian street, I had asked a stranger to help me; he had sent me to a special little store where I had met the son of a woman who had died the previous year, five thousand miles away! Two questions still linger in my mind? Was this just a coincidence? Did his mother from her heavenly home send me to bring some comfort to her son?

On another occasion, I received a message from Greece:

> *With profound grief, last night I witnessed our mother's death. She died peacefully. Please pray*

for the peace and rest of her soul. Your sister, Kiki.

Immediately, I called overseas. Kiki answered the phone with evident sadness in her voice. *Oh, how I wish you were here*, she sobbed. We talked extensively about Katerina and how good she had been as a mother to us. We both recalled endearing memories about her in our growing years.

Three days after her burial, I saw our mother in a dream. She had the small body of an eight-year-old girl; there were no arms or legs that I could see, but she had a youthful and beautiful face, and she was dressed in white. I picked her up and realized she had no weight. She looked at me with a radiant smile and said, *My son, put me on that sofa.* She pointed with glowing eyes. It was an old sofa in Kiki's house where she always liked to sit and do needlepoint. As I sat her down, my dream ended.

Now, years later, I'm still in a quandary: Did my mind improvise such a dream to defuse my grief? Or was that a message informing me that after death our souls do receive new bodies which are no longer physical? I rather believe the second, and as I think of both episodes, my faith in a loving God is forged. Someday all of us will find the answers. What we now perceive is like seeing "in a mirror, dimly," as Saint Paul claims, but in eternity, our perceptions will be perfected, when we will see reality "face to face" (1 Cor 13:12).

Epilogue

Now that we have considered the virtues of the soul, let's pause and consider this hidden treasure within you. When you reflect on each virtue's contribution to your inner self, you can feel glad and grateful. In your soul, you will find a true friend, a strong support, and your spiritual companion.

This soul is possibly the greatest gift that our Creator has given to human beings. It is invisible yet a good friend. Diligent self-care of this friend will help you maintain a healthy, fit, resilient, and happy existence. Caring for the soul isn't always easy, especially when our lives are busy and we have stressful jobs, not to mention the responsibility that comes with raising a family.

Some people become so consumed with technology that they neglect to make time for their own well-being. Such neglect invites stress and unnecessary pressure into our lives, and our body responds accordingly. Various health issues, ranging from digestion or an imbalance in one's metabolism to muscles tension or even tinges of memory loss, can lead to depression, negativity, and wrong decision.

No doubt you have heard or been told at some point in your life that *you only get out of something the amount of effort you put into it.* As we come to the end of this book, consider paying attention to your soul. To do this may be as simple as taking time each day to reflect on one of the virtues we have covered in this book; spending a few minutes in daily prayer and meditation; and being mindful of the gifts of the Holy Spirit—love, joy, peace, compassion, and forgiveness—the essence God's presence in our life that keeps us alive, healthy, content, and grateful for all the blessings we receive each day.